Paula is a vet
and a very good vet.
She opens the door
and she calls, "Next pet!"

1

Here comes a man.
He walks through the door.

He says, "My cat
has a very sore paw."

Paula has a look.
The paw is torn.

"Aha!" says Paula,
and takes out a thorn.

Yes, Paula is a vet
and a very good vet.
She opens the door
and she calls, "Next pet!"

Here comes a boy.
He walks through the door.
He says, "My little dog's
tummy is sore."

Paula tells the boy,
"Your dog is ill,
but she'll soon get better
if she takes this pill."

Yes, Paula is a vet
and a very good vet.
She opens the door
and she calls, "Next pet!"

10

Here comes a lady.
She walks through the door.
She says, "My rabbit
has a very long claw."

Paula tells the lady,
"The nail needs a clip."
Paula gets her scissors –
snip, snip, snip!

13

Yes, Paula is a vet
and a very good vet.
She opens the door
and she calls, "Next pet!"

Here comes a girl.
She walks through the door.
She says, "My mouse
won't run any more."

Paula has a look,
and she says, "I think
your mouse just needs
more water to drink."

All the morning,
Paula the vet
sees pet,

after pet,

after pet,

after pet.

More and more dogs,

more and more cats,

more and more rabbits

and mice

and rats.

Paula sees ordinary pets
all morning.
Paula feels bored.
Paula starts yawning.

"It's always the same,"
thinks Paula the vet.
"I wish I could see an
extraordinary pet!"

But Paula the vet
is a very good vet.
So she opens the door
and she calls, "Next pet!"

Here comes someone.
He walks through the door.
It's a very small boy. . .

with a **dinosaur!**